UNSEEN FORCES

BY

Manly Hall

FOURTH REVISED EDITION

Martino Fine Books
Eastford, CT
2019

Martino Fine Books
P.O. Box 913,
Eastford, CT 06242 USA

ISBN   978-1-68422-369-5

Copyright 2019
Martino Fine Books

Cover Design Tiziana Matarazzo

Printed in the United States of America On 100% Acid-Free Paper

UNSEEN FORCES

❖❖❖

BY

Manly Hall

❖❖❖

FOURTH REVISED EDITION

❖❖❖

HALL PUBLISHING COMPANY
944 West 20th Street
Los Angeles, California

CHAPTER I

THE CHILDREN OF THE ELEMENTS

The ancient philosophers peopled the elements of Nature with races and species unheard of by the average individual. The wise men of all ages have claimed that Nature works through intelligent forces and not through mechanical laws. Upon this hypothesis has been built the doctrine of the Nature Spirits and Elemental Larvae. Paracelsus, called the Swiss Hermes, and the greatest physician of modern times, has given us the most complete analysis of these strange creatures who live, move, and have their being unseen and unrealized by mortal man. Though we daily see their works, we have never learned to know the workers who, day and night, function through Nature's finer forces.

These elemental spirits may be divided into three groups:

(1) The elementals of the four elements or ethers which we commonly know as the Nature Spirits.

(2) The man-created elementals of the astral and mental planes.

(3) The Dweller on the Threshold, or the individual elemental.

THE FOUR ELEMENTS

According to the ancient doctrines, the tangible universe is composed of four principal elements. These four elements are under the rulership of the Lords of Form, who are sometimes referred to as the four-headed Cherubim. The four-headed Cherubim which stood at the gates of the Garden of Eden; the four-headed Cherubim which, with its brother creation, knelt upon the Mercy Seat of the Ark of the Covenant; the four beasts of the Apocalypse; the four aspects of the great Assyrian sphinx; the Babylonian man-bull—all are symbolic of these four primal elements.

From time immemorial man has divided form into four basic essences. These four essences are the basis of all things cognizable by human material body centers of consciousness. All things superior to these four essences can be cognized only by spiritual vision. All the numerous complex forms which appear in this world as the products of the geometrical outpourings of the Lords of Form, or the great body-building Devas, are the expressions of four streams of life. These are referred to as the rivers of life pouring out of the garden of the Lord, and they have as their source the great creative hierarchy which the ancients referred to as the Kings of Edom. Physical bodies are animated above cosmic root substance by these streams of life-giving ether. This ether is that part of the body of the Universal Logos (or something even higher which we do not know) which occupies the position of a carrier or container, for it passes through itself in four streams the powers of the creative Logos. From its essences are extracted the four creative principles which at the present time are the basis of the human fourfold vehicle: (1) physical or dense, (2) etheric or watery, (3) astral or fiery, (4) mental or airy.

These four vehicles, symbolized by the ancients as the arms of the cross, form the basis of the sacred doctrine of the crucifixion. Being the primal basis of bodies, these four are under the control of the body-building qualities and signs known as the four fixed signs of the zodiac. There are three crucifixions enacted in the zodiac: the cross of the four cardinal signs, the cross of the four fixed signs, and the cross of the four common signs. These, in turn, represent the three major crossings of the vital forces in the human body. The entire etheric world with its many crossing currents has its seat in the solar plexus and spleen of the human body. It is often referred to as the molten sea, or the laver of purification, for in its watery depths the soul in its pilgrimage to immortality must be washed. These four elements are the basis of, as well as the life behind, the four physical material elements—earth, fire, air, and water. The power from the unseen causal worlds works through the four material elements in order to express itself in bodies, cells, and molecular combinations.

As each kingdom in Nature has a series of lives evolving through it and is the plane of a great natural outpouring, so it is claimed that these four divisions of ether, expressing themselves in matter as the four elements, are inhabited by groups of intelligences evolving through these elemental essences. According to the ancients, these elementals are created out of a single substance—the ether or element in which they exist. They have no compound body and, therefore, are not capable of immortality, having no germinal life essence other than their respective elemental essence. On the other hand, being composed of only one substance, they are free from the destructive and inharmonious influences of the cross currents affecting compound bodies and therefore live for many hundreds —some of them for thousands—of years. Classical literature contains many references to these elementals. In Pope's poem, *Rape of the Lock*, the elementals play the most important part; in the Abbe de Villars' *Comte de Gabalis* (a remarkable book) there is also a very exhaustive thesis on these strange people of Nature. They are of varying shape and size, according to their work and duties. Their bodies also are of varying degrees of density, according to the element in which they work.

(Paracelsus and the Comte de Gabalis divide the Nature Spirits into four general classes: (1) *gnomes*, the earth spirits; (2) *undines*, the water spirits; (3) *salamanders*, the fire spirits; and (4) *sylphs*, the air spirits.)

THE GNOMES

Under the general heading of gnomes we find those creatures known as the tricksies, hobgoblins, elfs, forest-men, brownies, dwarfs, little old men of the rocks, and many other similar titles. The gnomes are the most dense of the Nature Spirits and consequently are more subject to the laws of mortality. They live in the element of earth and are said to work among the rocks and to some extent with trees and flowers. They are dwarf-like in stature, rather thick-set, with large heads and a waddling gait, their garments growing as an integral part of them. According to Paracelsus, they marry and have families, living in a strange world which the Norse people called *Elfheim*. They are said to have come out of the earth and still to penetrate it to its very core. They also live in caves and mold the stalactites and stalagmites. These little

8

people are often seen by children, who remain clair-voyant up to about the seventh year. In the forests they are sometimes seen storing up provisions for the winter. They are an industrious little people who are given charge of the molding and forming of earth. Under the direction of wiser ones, they have charge of all the solids, bones, and other tissues of the human body, working with them and restoring them. No broken bones would be set were it not for the assistance of the gnomes.

The king of the gnomes is called *Gob*—a name from which the word *goblin* is derived. It is said that one of these elemental kingdoms dwells at each of the four corners of creation; and the gnomes, who work with the most crystallized of all elements, have been given the northern corner of creation as their home. The ancients declared that the gnomes govern the secret treasures and hidden things of the earth and that those who would seek for material treasures hidden in Nature must first gain the support and assistance of the gnomes, who at will can either unveil them or so conceal them that they cannot be found. The gnomes are very miserly, greedy, and fond of good things to eat; on the other hand, they work incessantly, are very patient and faithful, and in our world would be called steady and temperate. Occasionally they meet in great conclaves in the heart of some dark forest or among the rocks, and from them comes that won-derful story of Rip Van Winkle in *The Legend of Sleepy Hollow*. A busy little people, they play a great part in the development of man, and assist him in his work. They work intuitively through the elements; and while they have a certain form of mentality, it is much inferior to ours. They are incapable of ex-pressing or manifesting themselves through any substance other than their own element. The hypothetical ether pervading solid crystallized substances as the first etheric essence is the only substance in which the gnomes can function.

Certain types of gnomes dwell in old ruined castles. This is one reason why old buildings are overgrown with vines and creepers, for the gnomes are eternally seeking to beautify Nature. They work in rocks and corals under the sea and also with the shell-fish. Some of them attain great size; others have the power of changing size at will, as long as they remain in their own substance. The majority, however, are much smaller than human beings and unprepossessing in appearance. Since they dwell in the darkness and gloom, the gnomes are said to have a certain effect upon human disposition and to govern the saturnine melancholia, gloom, and despondency.

THE UNDINES

Under the classification of undines are listed the nymphs, naiads, mermaids, sirens, harpies, sea-daughters, and sea-goddesses of the ancients. These are the elementals whose home is in the element of water—the oceans, lakes, streams, and rivers of the earth. Incidentally, they govern the liquids or vital forces of the human body. As the gnomes represent the sign of Taurus in the zodiac, so the undines represent Scorpio, having to do with the life and vital forces of Nature. They are reputed to be very beautiful, and in their realm beauty seems to be the keynote of power. They have many qualities similar to the gnomes, for they dwell in a world of their own. They are generally considered to be amicable and fortunate, and serve man in the spirit of love and sincerity. Like

the gnomes, they have their own rulers, who are sup-
posed to be individuals of an unusual degree of
superiority. Their supreme ruler, Necksa, they obey
and reverence very highly. All these beings have a
knowledge of God, revere Him, and seek to obey Him
in every way. The undines have been given the
western corner of creation and are said to whisper
sometimes through the west wind, which is the medium
of their power. They work with the creatures living in
the sea and also are said to have an important part
in the production of rain.

Mediæval philosophers (especially Paracelsus) held
the belief that storms were caused by battles between
the Nature Spirits; that the crossing of their qualities
resulted in great disturbances in the heavens which we
know as storms and upheavals. The undines are about
the same size as human beings, and are generally
symbolized as maidens draped in sea foam or riding
on the sea-horses or as mermaids. Being composed of
a subtler essence and a finer quality of ether, the
undines live much longer than the gnomes but are
also subject to the laws of mortality. They are specially
interested in plants and flowers, probably because the
etheric double of the plant is of the same type of
ether as their own. The undines are of a cheerful
disposition and their emotions are vital rather than
astral in quality. Being vital in temperament, they
exercise considerable influence upon the vital temperament of human beings.

THE SALAMANDERS

The ancients highly honored the salamanders, calling
them the Fire Kings because of their flaming appearance, their great strength and power, and the im-

portant part played by them in human affairs. No spark or fire can be lighted upon the earth without the assistance of a salamander, for they are the spirits of the fire. Those able to study the phenomena clair' voyantly can see these great fire kings twisting and turning in the flames, particularly during a great conflagration. Many of the ancients believed these fire salamanders to be gods, even claiming that their great emperors were the children of these fire kings. The salamanders have charge of the emotional essences of man and live in the third ether, which reflects the qualities of the astral plane, or the world of fire. They vary in shape and size, and are sometimes seen crawl' ing through the fire. They were known to the ancients as great giants in flaming armor who soar through the essences of the element of fire. They are very closely connected with every sacred organization that has fire upon its altar, and there is little doubt that they are identical with the flame-giants of Scandinavia. They are especially fond of incense, the fumes of which enable them to assume certain forms of bodies. The salamanders are the strongest and most dynamic of all the elementals. A great similarity exists between them and the Lucifer angels and also the great fire Devas of India. In volcanoes and the fire strata of the earth they are said to have their homes and to wield their authority. Their flaming king, *Djin,* is a glorious being, fierce and awe-inspiring, who rules them with a rod of flame. Though dangerous to human life, the salamanders, when properly understood, are great benefactors. They are hasty of action, tempestuous, and emotional but very energetic. Some of them assume tremendous proportions and resemble the giants of prehistoric times, while others are small and barely visible to the eye Their home is said to be in the south and they are felt in the warm winds of the equator. Their temperament is sanguineous and they influence to a certain extent all individuals with that temperament. If this quality is permitted to become the controlling power in life, the salamanders working through it confer upon all whom they thus unfluence tempestuous natures, fiery temperaments, and uncon-trollable passions. Because of the tenuity of the element in which they live, the salamanders are seldom seen. They live to an extreme age, many existing for thousands of years before being finally dissolved back into the primal essence from which they were differ-entiated.

THE SYLPHS

The inhabitants of the fourth ether (the finest and highest of all) are called the sylphs, or air spirits. They are also known as the riders of the night, the wind-born, the storm angels, the air-devas, the mind-born, and by many other names. The ancients believed their homes to be in the clouds. Deeper study how-ever, has proved that this group of elementals (who include the fairies and all those creatures with irides-cent wings referred to in children's fairy tales) really have their homes upon the mountain tops rather than in the air itself. The sylphs live and have their being in their own ether, and, like the gnomes, propagate and maintain themselves in a world of their own, building their air-castles out of that subtle element which is the reflector of the mental plane. They vary in appearance, some resembling human beings but with slightly different proportions. They are said to be mirthful, eccentric, capricious, and inconstant, darting hither and thither. They are always busy and work especially with the thoughts of living creatures. They assist in the airy elements of man's body, such as the gases and ethers which are generated in his own being, while the salamanders work through the blood and the fire elements of the body. The leader of the sylphs is called *Paralda,* who is said to dwell on the highest mountain of the earth. The sylphs are powerful and wield powerful influence upon all things in which air is an important factor. The next two thousand years will be an air age, in which the influence of the sylphs will be especially evident, and the conquest of the air will have a great deal to do with the discovery of these latent and concealed facts.

The ancients claimed that wars, plagues, fires, earth-quakes, and other cataclysms were caused by great armies of elementals who, marching in military array against each other, fought each other in these elements of Nature. Thus, thunder and lightning were said to be caused by battles between the sylphs and sala-manders, while rains and tidal waves were caused by the sylphs and undines. Movement of bodies in the earth, landslides, and internal rumblings were said to be caused by inharmony between the salamanders and gnomes. Generated out of the explosions of gun-powder, the salamanders hover over battlefields. As great armies of red flaming creatures they also feed upon human passion, obsessing the mind of man and finding expression through the respective ethers in his body.

The four groups—gnomes, undines, salamanders and sylphs—form the natural inhabitants of the etheric elements. Their labor is carried on through what is called the humidity body of both the earth and the

Planetary Logos, and also their corresponding poles in the body of the individual. In addition, there are several other groups of elementals, some the products of natural phenomena and others generated by man. Among these may be mentioned the thought and emotion elementals, ghosts, specters, the Dweller on the Threshold, and larvae. The latter group (known also as etheric shells) are the etheric bodies of individuals who in passing out at death have gone on to the astral plane. Casting off the etheric body soon after the physical form, they leave it behind in the ethers, where it slowly disintegrates. These shells are the basis of the greater percentage of mediumistic manifestations, a fact which can be determined only through an examination of the eyeballs of the medium. These shells also are often used by both elementals and larvae as temporary vehicles of manifestation as they float around in the ethers in process of disintegration. Due to the fine structure of these etheric shells, however, it often takes many years for disintegration to take place. Hence, a great host of etheric bodies float like chips of driftwood upon the sea of etheric humidity, discarded by their former owners who have long since passed on to other planes of life.

CHAPTER II

The Nature Spirits are sometimes visible to the human eye, but can be controlled only by those who are rulers of the elements in which these elementals live. Man's mastery of the elements therefore gives him dominion over these kingdoms. According to the ancients, the elementals were originally under the dominion of the Adamic man, and are always subject to the one who is master of their element. The elementals serve sincerely, though they do not realize or recognize the needs of the race they serve. Under the guidance of higher hierarchies, these creatures are the intelligent basis of natural phenomena and assist in implanting qualities and powers within the plant, the mineral, the animal, and man.

Many readers may not care to accept the reality of these entities. But as they form part of the great occult hierarchy and are the incarnation of natural principles, it is necessary that we give them a certain amount of attention and study. Under certain conditions these elementals have attached themselves to man and served him faithfully and well, as in the case of the dæmon of Socrates. Under other conditions they have been mistaken for angels, demons, and other supernatural larvae. They are said also to exist in essence in the chemicals of Nature. There are elementals not only of our earth and planetary chain but also of other planets and solar systems. The primary constitutional difference between the elementals and man is that the evolving life of which we are a part consists of complex organisms composed of spirit and its chain of vehicles, while the composition of the elementals is the one ether from which they are formed. Hence, the only evolution they can experience is the evolution of their own ether, from which they cannot dissociate themselves.

Practically all the occult wisdom of the world is based upon the knowledge of the four ethers and their powers as factors in the unfoldment of form combinations. The ethers in the bodies of the mineral, plant, animal, and man are the basis of the differentiation of these kingdoms of life. Without their vital principle (which is, in truth, the Hiram Abiff of Masonry) the temple-building of the ages could not go on. Among the ancient Oriental peoples, the doctrine of the four creations taught that from the body of Brahma, the concrete Deity, four children, representing the visible races of the earth, were born. From the feet of Brahma was born the black man, or the physical earth, which has been referred to as the footstool of God. From the thorax of Brahma was born the brown man, who represents the ether or ethereal outpouring of Nature. From the hands of Brahma (with their power of action) was born the red man, who represents the principles of motion and emotion, construction and destruction, action and reaction. From the mouth of Brahma was born the white man, the Brahmin, who is the spiritual and mental man. These four elements just described constitute the four outpourings from the Cosmic Egg. The Orientals sometimes divided the universe into five divisions, symbolized by the five fingers of the human hand. The Hindus recognize a fifth division extending from the root of the nose to the top of the head. The evolution of man consists in the passage of his consciousness through the four elements, which we find so wonderfully symbolized in the ancient initiations.

First initiation—*The slaying of the Dragon of Matter*. This is the triumph of the discrimination over the vehicles of Maya and the liberation from the chemical substances of Nature with their corresponding law of crystallization. This also consisted in overcoming the law of inertia and passing physically through a stone wall. This battle was won by means of the sword *Excalibur*, which is given to the king out of the waters of the vital ether by the hand of the undine.

Second initiation—*The rescue of the Pearl of Great Price from the ocean of living substances*. This Rhine-gold is guarded by the angels and the keepers of the vital forces of the body. Under the direction of the second group of elementals (already described as water spirits) are the vital forces of Nature, which they manipulate under the direction of higher hierarchies. This second initiation is accomplished by burning up the water with the flaming sword of the four-headed Cherubim which is turned upward into the brain. In this the candidate learns to cast the molten sea and receive the benediction of the holy water (which represents the vital forces of his own body), after which he passes under the sea and learns to solve the mystery of water which is born out of the thorax of Brahma.

Third initiation—*The passing of the Flaming Ring*. In this the candidate steps across the line between the two higher and the two lower elements in his effort to separate the soul from the animal body. This is told in the Northern legend of Siegfried and Brunhilde. The candidate receives the benediction of fire, incorporates the power of the salamanders into his conscious vehicle, and comes under the direct ray of Leo, the fire king of the temple. He learns to pass through flame and also to rule the flames in his own body. During this process he is taught to apply the gentle heat of the alchemist which, passing up the spine, hatches the egg of Brahma within himself, thereby loosening the serpent from its coil and turning its fire upward to the Tree of Life. Under this heading he takes the first mystic degree. If he remains here, he becomes a mystic and a power of the heart path of flame, and dons the crimson robe of Christ.

Fourth initiation. In this test the candidate gains the power of passing consciously through the spiritual atmosphere, and incorporates into his vehicle the active functioning power of the sylphs, or air spirits. He gains the power to read the atmospheric record of Nature and also of conscious functioning on the fourth plane of Nature through the assistance of the fourth elemental essence within himself. In the Norse myths he rides the eight-footed horse to heaven—the eight for many ages being symbolic of the path of the spirit fire in man. He thus combines these four elements in the power of mind, which is made available by the fourth ether, and is the highest form of consciousness which we have at the present time.

All these initiations are possible only through the interpenetration of the elemental essences with the organism of man. During these initiations he gains mastery over the elements and the various groups of intelligences which inhabit them. In our present work we are considering only one of these groups of inhabitants, namely, the Nature Spirits.

Briefly stated, the elements are as follows (beginning with the lowest):

1. Basic, atomic ether, (gnomes), expressing its highest phase in crystallization.

2. Humidic ether (undines), expressing itself as the water of life, the divine Mother Isis of all things.

3. The astral ether (salamanders), expressing itself in all motion and sense perception.

4. The mental ether (sylphs), expressing itself as the basis of memory perception and the reasoning intellect.

These four represent the channels for the expression of the forces of the four worlds of Nature through which man is evolving at the present time. *The ether is not the world itself, but is merely a substance capable of carrying or perpetuating that which is the product of some other sphere.* Ether was referred to by the ancients as the hypothetical mirror of eternity, because it mirrors the worlds of Nature into concrete form, vitalizing and impregnating this form with the sparks of life which it contains within itself.

When the hand of the priest is lifted in benediction, two fingers are raised and two are lowered. The two lowered fingers represent the elements of earth and water; the two raised fingers represent the elements of fire and air, while the thumb represents the Akasa or spirit. In this way the priest gives the benediction of the four ethers, without which consciousness is impossible, and the influx of which is the basis of growth, redemption, and regeneration.

CHAPTER III

THOUGHT FORMS AND
EMOTION GENERATED ELEMENTALS

It has been ordained that man, like his God, shall become a creator. The spark of life within him is capable of giving eternal life to the undifferentiated particles existing in Nature. In other words, in man is a touchstone which changes into a substance like itself all with which it comes in contact. As the universe is peopled by the sparks from the wheels of God, so the elements of Nature are peopled with the sparks flying out from the wheels of life, twisting and whirl- ing within the lower organisms of Nature. Man is a god in the making—he is much closer to godhood than he realizes or than it is safe for him to know. The infinite desire to create pulses through his blood as it courses through the being of Deity; every moment of his life he is expressing the God-like qualities of creation. Not only does he create his kind and perpetuate his species through natural law, but upon the higher planes of Nature he is also creative. As his physical organisms reproduce their kind, so there are other children also born out of his being.

Recalling the four creations from the body of Brahma, we may now say that from the symbolical substances of the feet of Brahma (material earth), the thighs of Brahma (ethereal water), the breast of Brahma (astral fire), and the brain of Brahma (mental air) are fashioned the quaternary vehicle by means of which the spiritual ego is able to function respectively in the physical, ethereal, astral, and mental worlds. Through the medium of the generative powers in the physical world, man assists in forming the physical bodies of his fellow creatures. He is likewise able to direct planes of substance for the expression of other waves of evolving life, purely physical. Upon the third world, where the red man was born out of Brahma, there pours forth from the Brahma in man a great stream of creatures built by himself—as much his children as the physical bodies produced in this world. He is as responsible for these as he is for his own flesh and blood which grows up around him in the form of his children and descendants. We do not understand this, because these children are invisible to the normal sight of the physical world. The trained clairvoyant, however, is able to see them, and realizes that as we are peopling this world with children who are to grow into its future citizens, so surely are we peopling the astral plane with the children of our emotions—strange fiery creatures born out of our own emotional body, with its great whirling vortex in the liver. This body is the Lion of the Cherubim, and from it there streams forth into the world the offspring of the emotional plane.

OUR ASTRAL CHILDREN

(The Astral World is called a plane in Nature)

Human passion, compassion, emotion, and desire are the qualities which attune the body of the individual with the corresponding body of the Macrocosmic Man. God—or Brahma, as we prefer to call Him— has a septenary constitution. For each one of His bodies there is a corresponding pole or vibratory vortex

22

in the human body, these poles being centers of activity which correspond to the greater plane centers in the Universal Man. By analogy, there is little doubt that the planets of our chain are the permanent seed atoms of the Universal Man and that each atom is the center of a septenary system of globes composed of varying degrees of density. In the Universal Man, these bodies are called planes of Nature; in the lesser man, these planes are called bodies. At the present time, we are able to cognize only the wave creation passing through the seven globes which are attuned to material creation. It is safe to say, however, that in the Greater Creation, Brahma created waves of life on each of His planes (or bodies) and that the invisible elements of Nature are peopled with races, rounds, chains, and globes, passing through the septenary chain of manifestation—none realizing or understanding the existence of any other order, or being understood, in turn, by any other. Since this is true of the Greater Man, and since the law of analogy is an unerring guide, we are safe in assuming that man (the lesser universe) is not only carrying on the work of physical creation, but also an elaborate series of astral and mental creations, which the trained seer is able to study at first hand and the attributes of which he is able to classify.

Following is a resume of some of the outstanding features:

1. There is a plane of Nature corresponding to each one of man's bodies. Evolution consists in lifting the center of life consciousness successively from one plane to another by the gradual attunement of consciousness with the vibratory rate of that plane.

2. In the Western world, the physical plane is the

world of reality, because the consciousness of its inhabitants is concentrated solely upon material things,
the sense centers being entirely enmeshed in the visible
and physically tangible.

3. The physical world is to us the only existing
reality because we cognize the external only through
the vibratory rates of sense perception; and our present
rate of sense perception attunes us with the plane of
the lowest—the feet of Brahma—the level of the
Sudra, or servant.

4. In Nature there is a world or plane (one of
the bodies of Brahma) to which man becomes attuned
through the vibratory rate of the emotional sutratmic
atom. The whirling of the atom produces a rate of
vibration and each of these seed atoms vibrates to a
different key. To one capable of understanding them
and whose senses have made the proper attunements,
these seed atoms intone a mystic chant, whose notes
sound like the thunderous tones of a colossal organ in
Nature. Never ceasing their wondrous pin-wheel
motion, they join the ensemble of the celestial sym-
phonies of marching spheres. In a lesser way, they sing
the chant sung by the planets, and thus breathe the
sacred name of the Most High, that wondrous Being
composed of all these sparks of life that robe themselves in this endless scroll of vibratory sound.

5. From the physical body of man there extends an
egg-shaped aura, with the large end at the bottom.
This aura, commonly called the astral body, is a series
of swirling emanations in which the rudiments of the
organs can be traced in spirals and pin-wheels of
colored light. This egg-shaped body extends from
twelve to fourteen inches beyond the physical form
and is the vehicle of conscious expression that attunes

man, the little god, to the emotions of his Creator. Like the ruddy planet Mars—which is its keynote— this body glows with opalescent shades and coloring with pink, violet, and orange predominating. This body is as much a part of our organism as the physical body, and we function in it many years after the death of our physical form.

6. This astral body expresses all the sentiments, emotions, desires, hates, fears, excesses, and active qualities of the human organism. From it pour perpetually into the astral plane of Nature the mancreated elementals which people this plane in the great universe.

7. The astral plane was divided by the ancients into two grand divisions—-*Karma Loka* and *Devachan*. These words express more adequately than any English words the qualities of this world. *Karma Loka* translated means primarily the world of Compensation. It has been identified by the religious organizations of Christianity with purgatory, and is composed of the three coarsest planes of the astral world. It is well for us to realize that the so-called purgatory of the ancients is many times finer in its atomic principles than the physical world and that it interpenetrates physical matter. Though we are unaware of it, the eternal flames of hell are now in our very midst, unseen and unrecognized but absolutely harmless, because at the present time we function at a different rate of vibration.

8. Into this lower division of the astral plane are poured the elementals generated by the emotions of man. Our hates and fears and excesses may thus be said to be pooled in the three lower planes of the astral world. There the clairvoyant is able to see the fruitage of human degeneracy and the children born

of the animal body of man. These creations are often strange contradictions of the things a person would have the world believe them to be, for they register not the polish but the secret excesses of his life. As streams of demons and monsters such as haunt the sleep of the opium fiend or flash before the eyes of the drunkard, we see the children born of the lowest side of God's fire world. They issue from us in a never-ending stream and feed this seething throng of fire beings that destroy each other in this world of darkness. This is indeed the Inferno of Dante. Here in *Karma Loka*, the land of sin, man must meet his creations face to face and confront the children of his vices.

9. Man little realizes the immortality that he is capable of conferring upon his creations. There is an apocryphal story of the Master Jesus how, when a child at play, He molded clay pigeons and, tossing them into the air, gave them life so that they could fly up into the heavens. In the same manner, each of us, with the power of immortality in his soul, is giving life to the substances of Nature—molding them into the expressions of our temperaments and personalities, and launching them to float for ages in the subtle essences of being and to carry with them the blessings or the curse with which we ourselves have endowed them.

THOUCHT FORMS

Thoughts are geometric outpourings of the mental body. They are germinated and vitalized through the union of the mental plane with the physical brain which, as father and mother, gives birth to the child—

a thought. In order to think, it is necessary for the entity to have in his being a center of conscious power, a sutratmic vortex, of the same rate of vibration as the mental plane. Around this he builds the mental aura which consists of an egg-shaped vehicle, sometimes with uniform ends and sometimes with the upper end slightly larger. This ovoid, being attuned to Saturn —the mind-born—is dark indigo in color, but pierced with the thought form of many colors and usually fringed with a fine hem of golden light, sometimes changing to green and orange. This body (which is the vehicle of consciousness on the mental plane) is the highest we are capable of building at the present time, the vortices of the higher bodies being as yet latent.

The Masters of Wisdom—the highest Initiates of our life wave—function in their mental bodies, which some of them are capable of molding into a close facsimile of the human form. This is the body from which issue the thought forms, strange geometric outpourings, and many-colored waves and rays. These are also the children of man; having created them, he is responsible for them, as he is powerless to prevent them from going forth in the spirit of their creator.

We are surrounded by our own emanation bodies, which are constantly pouring into the infinite reservoirs streams of energy both constructive and perverted. These streams of energy result from vitalizing our emotions and thoughts and thereby conferring upon them the power of our immortality.

DEVACHAN

In the Orient, *Devachan* is called the home of the Devas, a great race of spiritual creations, or rather higher astral creations, who never appear on the physical plane but who function continually in their astral bodies or occasionally in their mental bodies. The Devas are correlated sometimes with the salamanders, but this is incorrect, as the careful student readily comprehends. The ancients recognized three groups of these Devas: (1) the formless Devas of the higher mental planes, whose vehicles are formed of the cloudless night of the Arupa substance (abstract mental essence); (2) the embodied Devas, who are the great beings who dwell on the Rupa, or form-mental plane composed of concrete mind-stuff similar in texture to thought forms; and (3) the fire Devas, or the inhabitants of *Devachan,* the higher astral plane.

The Devas form part of that great group of spiritual entities who assist in carrying out the directions of the Planetary Logos. They are marvelous beings endowed with great wisdom, glory, and power, and they never appear on the physical plane. Their knowledge is apparently limitless, and to meet one is an unforgettable experience. The Devas form one group of the instructors of humanity on the higher planes of Nature. These beings are outpourings from the waves of creation, evolving as children thrown out of the superphysical bodies of deities. Some of them are called "skin-pore" creatures, others "fire-born"; in many of the ancient doctrines they were called "blood-born," and in still others, "children of thought."

As surely as these creatures are the mind-born Sons of God, so surely are the thought forms and astral elementals the mind- and fire-born sons of human beings. Man is responsible for these strange creatures who float around and battle for ages before they are finally dissolved in the essences of God's body. Had man the power of immortal creation, he would people the elements with these demons. But as yet he is only learning. In this is his salvation.

CHAPTER IV

GHOSTS AND SPECTERS

Besides the living inhabitants of the elements, there is another class of elementals commonly called *shades, ghosts,* or *specters.* We now group under a single heading as ghosts both decarnated spirits and the shells which float lifeless in the essences of the superphysical planes. This is incorrect, for in truth the word *ghost* (taken from the word *gust*) means a passing shadow or the reflection cast by the light upon the surrounding darkness. Jehovah, the God of form, like the Shiva of India, (the third aspect of the Trimurti) and Osiris (the third aspect of the Egyptian Trinity), is represented as the Lord of the Shades, or the shadows of the underworld. In reality, all bodies are ghosts, because they are phantoms of the real. That which is a shadow of the eternal is called a ghost or specter, and it has no reality save through the reflection of life upon substance.

Over graveyards at night there hang globes of phosphorescent light and wavy draperies of phosphorus; for the human body, when disintegrating, creates a luminous mist. The ancient peoples called this lumin-ous mist a shadow, or shade. It was also said that the shades of men walked the by-ways of their past, like Hamlet's ghost on the castle battlement. Generally speaking, we may divide the ghosts who walk in the night into two general classes.

First, there are the disintegrating bodies of decar-nated intelligences. Man dies not once in Nature but many times. He sloughs off not only a physical vehicle but later also an etheric body, an astral body, and lastly a mental body. These are cast off, the densest first, like the layers of an onion. When cast off from the spiritual monad, each of these shells floats in its own essence of being for a considerable time before entirely disintegrating, because the subtle essences of Nature preserve for many ages the bodies of which they are composed in the same way that alcohol pre-serves flesh. The essences of Nature are filled with slowly decomposing bodies which were cast off after their experiences had been incorporated into the spiritual organisms of man.

In these essences of Nature there also dwell creatures who take upon themselves these slowly dissolving bodies as a player dons a masquerade costume or wears a mask. These masqueraders are usually the elementals of the ether. The ghosts seen are usually etheric bodies from which the spiritual consciousness has fled, and they either drift past the vision of man like a derelict floating on the sea, partly animated by the subtle substances of the ethers, or they have been vitalized (sometimes humanized) by an intelligence from one of these subtle planes.

People say, "The vision I saw was not a floating corpse; it moved, it raised its hands, and looked at me." They do not realize that this drifting, moving mass of etheric protoplasm is floating upon the sur-face and in the midst of a sea of ether. If one could walk upon the ocean bottom and see the great waving branches of seaweed dimly outlined in the pale green light, he would see a lifeless substance, incapable in itself of locomotion or animation beyond the vital principle of propagation. This substance sways and

31

moves, twists, and turns as though alive. Long streams of seaweed, resembling the body of a boa constrictor, wave long sinuous branches in the same way that the ghost of the night points its finger or directs its glassy eye toward the victim of the vision. The movement is not initiated, however, within the thing which we see moving, but is the result of the movement of external forces.

Only those who have been conscious on the lower planes of the ethereal worlds can understand what it means to see these floating shells, drifting, drifting, ever fainter, until many years later—sometimes cen- turies—a strange face, so faint as hardly to be visible, marks the final disintegration of the ethereal specter

The etheric plane is really part of the physical world. It is tied to the physical globe because in reality it is the mold into which the dense body is cast, just as the physical anatomy of man is really molded into the etheric double. The etheric body is purely a physical substance but far more attenuated than the solids, liquids, and gases which we see. It is more or less tied to the physical body, sometimes disintegrating with it, but usually remaining differentiated from the substance of the astral world. The etheric body hovers over or near the grave where the body has been placed and sometimes leads to an earthbound condition. To prevent this possibility, the ancient occultists cremated the physical body. When this is done nothing remains to tie the higher intelligence to matter, the body having been entirely reduced to basic inorganic substance.

The first dawning of etheric vision (which is really nothing more than an extension of physical sight ar d not clairvoyance as some imagine) brings man into the world of specters—the borderland between the physi al and true superphysical worlds. Here he sees these forms in flowing draperies, formed out of the fine atoms of this world, seething and twisting, Dantesque fashion, in endless clouds. Millions of them stretch as far as the eye can reach, floating in groups or wavy lines in the sea of ether in which they are preserved. In the endless march of time they are slowly reduced, however, the atoms returning to the etheric world in the same manner that physical atoms finally return to dust. And as the physical atoms are incorporated again into ever-changing bodies and as that which was once in the body of man may next appear in the organism of plant or animal, so the ether which once was attracted by the centers of etheric consciousness to build a body, when dispelled by time, finally gathers itself into new forms. The particles of man's own etheric body are made from the disintegrating atoms of the millions of ghosts that have been floating in the ethers since eternity began. To this sea of ether the physical body will be returned when its labor is completed and the records which man has implanted in it and which are necessary for his soul growth have been extracted therefrom and incorporated into his higher vehicles.

Man has a body in each of the worlds of Nature which he has now connected up in his fourfold consciousness. The whole gamut of his expression—as manifest through form, growth, motion, and thought—are inspired by a complete organism, which in man is called a body and in the Grand Man a plane of Nature. Each one of these bodies functions on its own respective plane. Man is born into each one of these planes as the sutratmic atom descends and by the law of attraction assembles a body upon that plane. This body grows in a natural and progressive manner.

Then as he slowly sloughs off his vehicles in the decarnate state until finally only the monadic atom remains
upon the Arupa plane, he discards each of these bodies.
These discarded bodies thereupon become ghosts, or
shells, in the superphysical world just as the physical
body, when the spiritual ego has departed, becomes a
lifeless thing, preserving the shape of the living creature but without consciousness or intelligence.

This process had for its ancient symbol the moon
which is, in truth, a ghost, its intelligence having in-
carnated into the earth. It is a dead, lifeless shell, but
impelled by the power of the great disintegrator in
Nature, which is the Lord of the Ghost or Specter;
in other words, the Regent of the Moon.

Again, there is the earthbound spiritual consciousness which sometimes visits the living, but in this
case usually through the lower astral body. Consequently, it is never seen save when the individual is
partly asleep. People who have seen these specters
always affirm by all they hold dear that they were
wide-awake. The consciousness *is* wide-awake but
functioning at the moment in the lower astral body.
Hence, the physical body does not move during a
vision. People are incapable of standing up and ap-
proaching the specter. They think and are alive and
awake, but always in a dreamlike state in which they
are partly under the dominion of sleep. At this time
the physical body is in repose and the lower physical
qualities do not intersect or express themselves. Then
many people become slightly clairvoyant and see the
ghosts and specters of this world. The specter usually
takes a form outlined in gray, hooded in a dun-colored
or gray garment, and surrounded by a bluish-gray
light. After the decarnate person has been absent

34

from the physical plane for some years, the lower part of the body becomes merely a hanging drapery and finally vanishes altogether, because the higher astral plane preserves only the consciousness of the face. These specters usually appear because of some strong earthly ties such as jealousy and wrong-doing. Great love or great hate also draws them. By his avarice, therefore, the miser is recalled to his treasures. These are the phantom forms which curse old castles with their presence like the famous ghosts of Hampton Court and the ghost of Hamlet's father.

Once they are freed from the pangs of conscience or unfinished work, these specters disappear, because the consciousness dies out of the astral body and this body becomes merely a shell. The shell is then often assumed by elementals which continue to haunt the places where the spirit itself once did. A great percentage of the visions seen by mediums are merely these etheric shells vitallized by an elemental of the astral or etheric worlds. The earth-binding ties of narrow concepts, ignorance, one-pointedness of purpose or similar attitudes can be found in numerous instances. For months after the close of the late World War, soldiers on both sides who had died fighting still rose from the battle-field and fought in the ethers, wholly unconscious of the fact that they were dead. They maimed and destroyed each other, cursed and swore, and lived again among the bursting shells and shrapnel just as in former days. Still others wander among the forests of crosses in the great graveyards of Flanders and France, wondering after many years of death what has happened to them. The sea is still peopled with phantom ships whose crews, long since dead, still sail for the port which they were never able to reach alive. Among the ancient galleons on the etheric plane the old Spanish buccaneer still counts his gold, tied by the bonds of materiality and selfishness to the world of which he no longer is a part. The dope den is still peopled by the spirits of those who died slaves to its curse and who come back again to inhale its fumes and live in its filth. Like great vampire bats, they seek to gratify again the passions of their former earth lives by seizing the minds and souls of the living and obsessing them still here.

All these facts teach a great lesson. The answer to the problem of the earthbound is twofold. The first is right living and the second is *non-attachment.* Those who have done their best in this world need not worry nor come back to beg forgiveness, nor haunt the footsteps of those they wronged, waiting for liberation. Those who are not attached to the things of this earth go straight about their Master's business in other worlds as well, and go on and on fulfilling their duty. Then, again, if the people of this world would in spirit and in truth release the dead, they would not be surrounded by the specters who wail and pray, held by a force they cannot understand. When we weep for the dead, when we long for them to come back, we draw them from the Master's work and surround ourselves with phantoms that can never return but whom we can hold and divert from their life duty.

This shell, floating in the ether and in the lower worlds of the astral plane, can no more help or guide us in our search for salvation that a corpse could save us here. These shells are the things most often seen in visions. They are obsessed by lower elementals and the larvae of the lower astral plane. They rap on the table and tilt the chairs, they materialize their fruit and paint their pictures, and men foolishly make gods out of entities that are not even human. Let the student investigate these worlds for himself; or, if he is incapable of investigating them, let him learn the great truth that man owes no allegiance to that which he does not know. To his God he owes only the allegiance which his dawning consciousness has shown him that God deserves. Only with perfect conscious-ness will come perfect understanding and perfect co-operation with Nature's workings. The ghosts of old graveyards and the specters of a dream should be sent back into the planes from whence they came, where as shells they will float until eternity dissolves them or, if still the vehicle of consciousness of the spirit, be liberated to learn the lessons of the new world wherein they are. There, unhindered by human emotion, they will absorb the fruitage of their respec-tive bodies and build it into an eternal body—the temple of the soul—which is the crowning jewel, the great achievement of human evolution.

CHAPTER V

THE DWELLER ON THE THRESHOLD

Character and those qualities which are really the measure of human consciousness are not brought with the primitive germ of being out of the Infinite, but are the fruitage of experience and the mellowing that comes with spiritual age. The Primal Spark—the Unborn Deathless Thing in each organism— knows itself not, save by those bodies that it has built through contact with the inferior worlds, which we call the realms of form. The First Spark, this divine germ of spirit, makes possible all growth and expression; but growth, in the true spiritual understanding of the word, is the result of acceptance into the consciousness of the evolving atoms of those diverse factors which we group together under the heading of *experience* and without which the spirit cannot improve its primal lot.

The world that we know is the Kindergarten of spirit. Here child-souls in the making are instructed in realities by means of unrealities. As the cutting out of paper dolls and making of little ships from strips of paper is the first step in the education of a child, so things apparently very far from truth mold in a mysterious way the character of man into the paths that will later lead him to wisdom. Few here realize that *they are on probation in this world,* but such is the case. We are forced to hug the spokes of the wheel of illusion until, like the child in school, we outgrow our class and are promoted to a higher. As there are children in school who never seem to learn and who stay year after year in the same grade, so those who do not master the problems of the greater school of life must remain involved in matter until they realize the plan and (what is vastly more important) live in accordance with the reality they have discovered.

At the present time, all growth is carried on through the physical body. All the higher vehicles express themselves through this medium and are molded by the application made of their respective forces in the material world. Let us list them and describe how they are influenced:

The Mental Body. This is the highest vehicle man has at the present time, save a few very highly advanced Adepts and Masters who function consciously in the Buddhic body. In the majority of people, the mind body appears as a yellow cloud around the head and shoulders. The greater the thought force of the person, the more completely organized the mental body becomes. The brain is its vehicle in matter and the development of this superphysical body depends entirely upon the exercise of thought force—not upon other entities but upon solution of the problems of life in accordance with the faculties of reason and logic.

The Astral Body. This body is much older than the mind and is therefore much more perfectly developed. It finds expression through the fire in the human blood. The emotions, passions, and reactions with which man excites his organisms are expressions of this astral body. The heart, as an organ of influence over the destiny of consciousness, expresses the qualities of the astral body; and the mastery and directing of the emotional forces constitute the build ing of the astral soul body in man. The emotions are always swayed by extremes, and it is the balancing of opposites and the mastery of extremes here in life that molds the astral body into a permanent vehicle for the expression of spirit.

The Physical Body. This vehicle, composed of the chemical dense form and the etheric (or vital) double, is in principle the oldest of man's connections with the external universe and forms at this time the focusing point for all of the other bodies. The efficiency of this body measures the expression of all the higher vehicles. This shell forms the positive connection between the school of material experience and the subtle forces which man is seeking to unfold. Through this body and its expression all growth is now being carried on. When the inventor first outlines his idea, it must be adapted to practical needs and modified to meet the requirements of manufacture. In the same way, it is in the physical world that the schemes of the consciousness are put to practical test. Thus the physical world becomes the testing field of life, and only those who pass through it and upon its anvil translate their theories into practicalities are capable of really knowing the efficiency of their ideas.

We may now consider some of the expressions by which we have learned to judge the characters and lives of those with whom we come in contact. These are not gifts of the immortal spirit but rather the harvest from the fields of life when it has been lived intelligently. We know these as soul qualities:

Virtue. Virtue is innocence transmuted into intelligent realization of moral right. This can be accomplished only as the result of experience.

Continuity. The faculty of developing a certain line of reasoning and carrying it to a successful conclusion, without allowing outside interests or desires to divert the mind, is the result of long ages spent in mastering mental forces and developing will to the point where it becomes dictator of the emotions.

Discrimination. This is the ability to select from a number of apparently equal, yet diverse, possibilities that which is most suitable for the needs of the organ-ism. Experience is the only way by which far-sighted-ness on practical problems can be evolved.

Balance. The power to remain unmoved by passing conditions is gained by a careful analysis of life and the realization that the world we live in is to be studied and analyzed but never assumed as a reality. Man can never renounce that which he believes in or that which to him is a reality. He must be beyond the veil before he can be free from mundane illusions.

Wisdom. Understanding is always the product of actual experience. The philosopher with his gray hair and bent shoulders has lived life until he knows its ways and by-ways and can therefore assist others to a better understanding of Nature's realities. Age in soul power alone brings mellowness, which is the basis of wisdom.

Experience also confers many other qualities, some apparently good and others evil. Many feel that to wallow in the mire of sin is a great mistake; others believe that God must have some way of instructing His children better and easier than by forcing them to battle in darkness for their salvation. This must ever be an open question that each must settle for himself. All around us are thousands in the mire of degeneracy. A large part of our population is morally or physically unclean. It is too late to warn against mistakes such as all make and most uphold, so all that remains is to assist those who have fallen to get back on their feet and learn from their sorrows to avoid the pitfalls next time. No law can be passed that will make people good, but suffering makes people careful when advice is ignored; sorrow and disappointments make us think when warnings are permitted to pass unheeded. In this way man learns through his experiences, when he refuses to listen to anything else. The annals of life show that our greatest sinners have made our greatest saints, not because they made mistakes but because they learned through experience to correct them. We should all thank God that we have the power to suffer, for through pain great souls are born. Adversity overwhelms the sluggard, but galvanizes the soul into action and gives incentive to those who seek to achieve. Adversity disciplines the spirit and tests the resolve. With the mastery of adversity, courage is born.

We should thank God for our adversary, for he gauges man's true worth. "What would I do under certain conditions," is a question each should ask himself. Few of us know; and fewer still would do in a moment of extremity the thing planned at leisure. Place people in various positions, and then and there they judge and measure themselves before the world. They need neither accuser nor defender; their actions are the gauges of their souls, and their souls tell their age in the cosmic scheme of things as no protestation or profession could possibly do. Actions and attitudes are proofs; words are merely expressions of emotion which are seldom dependable. Man often argues with himself to prove things that he honestly knows are untrue. Usually the human animal convinces himself of the reality of the falsehood before he can possibly prove it to another. In fact, he seldom proves it to any save himself.

THE BUILDING OF THE SOUL

At the present time we use the two words *soul* and *spirit* as though they meant the same thing. This is not correct. "The soul that sinneth it shall die." (Ezekiel 18:4). Spirit does not die.

In occult philosophy, spirit is that ever-existing essence which is the immortal part of all created things in any of the seven worlds that manifest as a cosmic scheme. Spirit is indestructible, uncreated, and the germ of divinity in all manifesting creations; it is the God in you, the eternal permanence, the triple spirit of being.

Soul is the garment of spirit; it is the fruitage or essence of all the experience gained by manifestation in the concrete words of mind stuff, astral material, and physical substance. In a spiritual sense, man can only be clothed in his virtues. Hence, *the attainment of this golden garment of the soul is the real reason for life*. Incident is valueless, save for the impression that it leaves upon the nature of the one passing through it. By an occult process this impression is molded into the soul body as another thread in the seamless robe of the spiritual Bridegroom. In Nature nothing is lost, and this vehicle, created by the assimilation of experience since the time millions of years ago when the consciousness was first differentiated, is called the soul —the molder of destiny—the mentor that must be consulted when important decisions are to be made. The soul measures man's standard of right and wrong in the scale of things known. It is the basis of judgment and the inspiration behind the voice of conscience. Therefore, we ask with the seer of old, "What shall it profit a man if he gain the whole world and lose his own soul?"

Upon the soul are etched all the various actions and reactions that make up life. Therefore, the soul is essentially dual in its nature—that which registers successes and that which registers failures. The things which we have done well become our guardian angels, guiding and inspiring us to further achievement; while those things wherein we have sinned become our menacing accusers, ever confronting us with the responsibility for our own mistakes.

At the doors of the Eastern temples stand two dogs—one laughing and the other leering. They represent our own virtues and vices which we all must pass when we seek to enter the path that leads to Perfection. These two qualities—the good and the evil within ourselves—are ever with us. One points to heaven and the other ever stands as the great problem. The beast is still part of our nature and will remain so until we transmute the strength of the adversary into the inspiration to greater victories over self.

This adversary within, this accumulation of unpaid Karma, this Body of Sin, this ever-present obstacle, this spirit of negation, this ever-menacing figure of the evil in our own natures, was called by the ancients THE DWELLER ON THE THRESHOLD.

CHAPTER VI

THE PASSING OF THE DWELLER

The first great step in the ancient initiations was passing the terrifying monster that dwells on the border line between the physical and the spiritual worlds. The Children of Light were told that they could "never go forth into distant lands" or "earn the wages of Master Builders" until they faced with courage and resolution the invisible demon that dwelt ever with them and sought to awaken within themselves the subtle forces of which he was composed. Most people do not meet this fearful figure until at the time of death the intelligence functions for a brief time on that borderland of life and death, so-called, which is its dwelling place. There he crouches—the thing built by the sins of the flesh and the crimes committed in darkness—a specter of unearthly terror, the sum total of perversion, the aggregate of misused force and per- verted talents. Have we ever stopped to think that the things we do unwisely will sometime confront us like accusing judges and bar our way to the light that we will some day recognize and seek to serve?

Far back when man first sinned, this creature was born and cried out from the blood of the first of God's children that was slain. Hate and fear, jealousy and greed, passion and lust, thoughtlessness and crime —all these have fed it until today man carries with him an all-powerful thing reared and nursed by the worst that is in him, a beast-like demon ever spurring him on to crime and perversion, ever tempting him through the medium of habit to sink back into the

45

mire of degeneracy out of which he is crawling so painfully.

This is the Guardian of the Threshold. We have never seen him but every day we are fighting him, struggling to free ourselves from the coils of sin which are his manifestations. Every time we master an unworthy trait of character, we are passing the Dweller on our threshold; for we are divided from the world of spirit by our sins, and when we master our own mistakes by doing right where we did wrong before, sin becomes less of an obstacle. Finally we are able to face this creature for the last time, and among the ethers of the higher world struggle with the dragon of Karma until at last we vanquish him and, bathing in his blood, become immortal; for energy is the blood of the Dweller and he is built of the energy we have wasted or misused.

The Dweller differs from the elementals and Nature Spirits in this respect: the latter are a separate creation in themselves, floating about and living in the etheric essences; the Guardian, however, is attached to man and never leaves him. It grows or diminishes with the sins of the individual of whom it forms a part. *The Guardian of the Threshold is really the sin-body of all creatures who have individual intelligence.* Although man is the only intelligent creature that we know, there are many others in Nature. The planet Mars is the sin-body of the Solar God and is therefore His threshold Guardian, but the Deity has transmuted this power into the dynamo of the solar system.

Those who would serve their God safely and join the company of the immortals must first master their own sins. The price of entrance into the Temple is the conquest of our own lower natures, for we cannot serve both God and mammon. To force one part of the nature to develop spiritual powers while another side of the nature is a servant to vice and material things, is to invite insanity and death. There-fore, before one takes the true path of discipleship, he must have a long talk with himself and see how many of the elements of his lower nature he is allowing to tie him to earth. Then begins the great battle so often symbolized in the religious ceremonials of the ancients, which must result in the death of the lower nature—the Dweller. From the ashes of the flaming conflict the higher nature rises and becomes one with the spirit of light. This is the mystery of the cruci-fixion, and the inner meaning behind the third degree of the Masonic rite. On a smaller scale, it is played out in life every day, but at last it must be boldly faced and a decision made.

THE SINS OF THE FLESH

So long as any of the following traits are left in his nature, man has no right to seek first-hand know-ledge on spiritual subjects. This does not mean that he should not study, but he must keep away from occult activities that will work upon his superphysical nature and organisms. All of the following vices build and strengthen the power of the Dweller:

Hate	Anger	Selfishness	Pride
Fear	Sorrow	Egotism	Attachment
Greed	Passion	Dislikes	Contention
Excitement	Lust	Sulkiness	Argument
Emotionalism	Dishonesty	Lying	Demands

All students are subject to these failings. That is to be expected and there is no special disgrace in hav-ing them, for only the gods are without fault. Mayhap even they err sometimes; *but until these problems have been honestly faced and worked out, no one has the cosmic right to dabble in those things which lie behind the veil that divides this world from the invisible.* These are responsibilities we must meet and tests we must face, and our usefulness depends upon how we meet and master them; for every one of these faults makes us useless to the Great Ones who so greatly need help from the world of men.

What kind of a universe would we live in if our gods were subject to the failings listed above? If the sun should be subject to fits of anger, or the Masters begin to run things according to their own egotistic fancies, what would happen to us? If we aspire to positions of trust, we, too, must be as passionless, patient, and kind as the gods themselves. *No one ever reached the state of mastership other than by passing the Guardian of his lower nature and transmuting into creative powers the sins which give the Dweller his power.*

THE THREE STEPS

There are three distinct steps in the attainment of wisdom, and all growth must take place in accordance with these steps. If man really desires the boon of wisdom, he must be willing to accept it as the gods have seen fit to bestow it. The student must prepare himself for the influx of wisdom. This he does through right thought, right action, and right attitude.

Right thought is the open mind, ready to consider all things; a humble mind willing to receive the crumbs from the feasts of the wise; a charitable mind condemning none but itself; a far-sighted mind capable of seeing good in all things and ultimate good for all things.

48

Right action consists of proper care of the body, proper exercise, and a proper place in the great material battle of life. Man grows by contacting growing things. When he is able to contact all forms of life pleasantly, with consideration, with the heart of the helper, and with the mind of the student, he grows.

Right attitude means that everything is undertaken in the spirit of love, truth, and a sincere, unselfish desire to assist in making the world a better place in which to live. Right attitude means cheerfulness, hopefulness, and co-operation with all that is seeking to grow. It means consideration for all, even when they disagree with us, realizing that man must not work for man but for God, and that each has his separate account.

Having prepared himself for the coming of wisdom by cleansing his body, broadening his mind, and opening his heart, he must then apply himself to the task of digesting the knowledge that comes to him. The arrangement of facts so that they will be of practical use to the world is no small task. Much that we hear from occultists is of no value in solving every-day problems. While technical knowledge is necessary to a teacher, it must be presented in a way that will serve; otherwise, it might as well remain unsaid. The second step is the actual coming of wisdom itself, and this in turn prepares the way for the third stage.

Having prepared for and received the light, the third stage is that of using knowledge in the best and most convincing way. This is no child's play; it requires the wisdom and understanding of the gods themselves. People take the spiritual sciences too lightly. *They do not realize that the enlightened ones are picked from the very cream of the earth.* The brightest minds, the most beautiful souls, and the greatest successes are the ones chosen to serve with the band of Spiritual Ones. Modern occultism is filled with failures who were never of any value to themselves or to anyone else. If these scatter-brains think for a moment they are going to be lifted up in a few short months or years, they are very much mistaken. *The Masters use only the worthy ones.* What are we or what can we do that makes us worthy to ask for spiritual assistance in the employment office of God? What are our references? What letters of recommendation do we bring from our last employer, our friends, our world?

The following case illustrates what the Guardian of the Threshold means:

Mrs. X, an elderly lady is such a gossip that she is without a friend on earth. No one dares to speak in her presence. She has been married twice, but both homes have been broken up. She blames others, but all who know her realize that she is the one responsible. She has an ungodly temper, a sour disposition, and a body filled with acidity due to improper food combinations. She spends most of her time regretting unfortunate conditions of years ago, feeling that the world is against her. She will not believe that she is selfish, and she spends all her time telling what she knows. She expects everyone to agree with her and calls them fools when they do not. One minute she wants to embrace and the next she wants to kill those near her. She prays and meditates daily, and asks for spiritual enlightenment. She sees visions and believes that the creations of her mind are true, which is quite impossible. She is just one of countless thousands who expect illumination as their birthright and spirituality as a legacy. They do not realize that the Masters must have people who can do things. This lady could not earn five dollars a week in the material world, for she is a liability wherever she is, but she believes that she is valuable enough to God for Him to send one of His Masters to teach her against her own will the things she would not understand. *Those who want illumination are many, but few are worth the effort Nature must make in order to change their lives and produce something useful.*

An analysis of this lady shows that she has the following faults:

1. She is an incurable egotist.

2. She is a pessimist.

3. She has a violent temper. This temper poisons her blood.

4. She is selfish. The Masters are the opposite—altruistic.

5. She is emotional. She wastes energy, which is a crime.

6. She has a neglected body. God will not dwell in a temple that is not kept clean and free of disease.

These six faults comprise the Dweller on her Threshold. They stand between her and all the beautiful things she wants to be. *God will not remove these things from her, but will give her the thing she longs for when she proves her worth by mastering her own nature and awakening to her mistakes.* God makes a pact with man. If man will prepare the temple of his own life, the Father will take up His dwelling in it and be the light of that temple. Let us ask nothing of God until we have done our part; let us not try to gain spirituality until we have built our tabernacle according to the Law given to the Children in the days when the earth was young.

THE SPHINX

Who has fathomed the mystery of that expressionless face gazing out into the desert toward the place of the rising sun? That creature with the body of an animal is the sin-body of man—the Guardian of the Threshold—and, like the true constitution of man, it is unknown to the majority of people. Before the candidate can go forward in the spiritual work that he was ordained to do, he must wrest the secret of sin from the silent watcher. By concentration and consecration he must correct and master one after another of his own vices, until he can offer to the service of the Masters a life without a blemish. Then he will be accepted. But few there are who want a life without blemish. All want power, but how few can take the sword of quick detachment and plunge it through the heart of that leering specter—their own lower nature—the Dweller on the Threshold!

CPSIA information can be obtained
at www.ICGtesting.com
Printed in the USA
BVHW071925100822
644253BV00004B/742